Prayers
and Poems for
Christmas

Because the beginning
shall remind us of the end
And the first Coming
of the second Coming.

T. S. Eliot

IDEALS PUBLICATIONS INCORPORATED
Nashville, Tennessee

ACKNOWLEDGMENTS

ALMIGHTY GOD, HEAVENLY FATHER and O HEAVENLY FATHER from *THE BOOK OF COMMON PRAYER* (1928) of the Episcopal Church. Used by permission. BY THE SHINING OF A STAR and O GOD OF PEACE from *BOOK OF COMMON WORSHIP*, ©1946 The Board of Christian Education of the Presbyterian Church in the United States of America. Used by permission of Westminster John Knox Press. FOR OUR CHILDREN and WINTER from *TOWARD JERUSALEM* by Amy Carmichael, copyright ©1936 Dohnavur Fellowship (Fort Washington, PA: Christian Literature Crusade; London: S.P.C.K.). Used by permission. A CHRISTMAS PRAYER, JOSEPH, and THE ROAD TO CHRISTMAS by Grace Noll Crowell, used by permission of the author's estate. A CHRISTMAS WISH and I DO NOT ASK OF THEE by Edgar A. Guest, used by permission of the author's estate. A CHRISTMAS CAROL from *WHEN DAY IS DONE* by Edgar A. Guest, copyright ©1921 by The Reilly & Lee Co., used by permission of the author's estate. A PRAYER from *BE STILL AND KNOW* by Georgia Harkness, copyright ©1953 by Pierce & Washabaugh. Used by permission of the publisher, Abingdon Press. ONLY AN HOUR by Robinson Jeffers, used by permission of Jeffers Literary Properties. O SIMPLICITAS reprinted from *THE WEATHER OF THE HEART* by Madeleine L'Engle, ©1978 by Crosswicks. Used by permission of Harold Shaw Publishers, Wheaton, IL 60189. FOR A RENAISSANCE OF FAITH by Peter Marshall from *MR. JONES, MEET THE MASTER*, edited by Catherine Marshall. Copyright ©1949, 1950, 1977, 1978, 1982. Reprinted with permission of Fleming H. Revell. THE DAY AFTER CHRISTMAS; FOR CHRISTMAS THE YEAR ROUND; ON A WINTER'S DAY; and THE WONDROUS SPELL OF CHRISTMAS by Peter Marshall from *THE PRAYERS OF PETER MARSHALL*, edited by Catherine Marshall. Copyright ©1949, 1950, 1951, 1954, and 1982. Used by permission of Chosen Books, a division of Baker Book House. A PRAYER from *THE GREATEST OF THESE* by Jane Merchant. Copyright ©1954 by Pierce & Washabaugh. Copyright renewal ©1982 by Elizabeth Merchant. Used by permission of the publisher, Abingdon Press. WE THANK THEE, HEAVENLY FATHER from *THINK ABOUT THESE THINGS* by Jane Merchant. Copyright ©1956 by Pierce & Washabaugh. Copyright renewal ©1984 by Elizabeth Merchant. Used by permission of the publisher, Abingdon Press. A CHRISTMAS PRAYER by New York Life Insurance Company, ©1982 New York Life Insurance Company, New York, NY. All rights reserved. Our sincere thanks to the following authors whom we were unable to contact: Robert Merrill Bartlett for WINTER, from *BOYS PRAYERS, THE ASCENDING TRAIL* by Robert Merrill Bartlett, published by Association Press; Thomas Curtis Clark for THE CHRISTMAS HOPE; and Amos Russell Wells for THE INN: THE LANDLORD SPEAKS A.D. 28.

Editor, Nancy J. Skarmeas; Copy Editor, Michelle Prater Burke; Electronic Prepress, Amilyn K. Lanning

Copyright ©1995 by Ideals Publications Incorporated, Nashville, Tennessee

Printed and bound in the U.S.A.

ISBN 0-8249-4074-1

Designed by Gore Studio, Inc.
Film Separations by WebTech Inc.
Printed by RR Donnelley & Sons, Inc.

Contents

Christmas Families
4

Christmas Blessings
32

Christmas Faith
54

Christmas Journeys
76

Christmas Gifts
98

Christmas Adoration
118

Christmas Peace
134

Christmas Families

And in the sixth month the angel Gabriel was sent from God unto a city of Galilee, named Nazareth, To a virgin espoused to a man whose name was Joseph, of the house of David:

and the virgin's name was Mary. And the angel came in unto her, and said, Hail, thou that art highly favoured, the Lord is with thee: blessed art thou among women...behold, thou shalt conceive in thy womb, and bring forth a son, and shalt call his name JESUS. He shall be great, and shall be called the Son of the Highest: . . . and of his kingdom there shall be no end.

LUKE 1:26-33

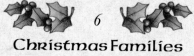

Christmas Families

The Wondrous Spell of Christmas

 e thank Thee, O God, for the return of the wondrous spell of this Christmas season that brings its own sweet joy into our jaded and troubled hearts.

Forbid it, Lord, that we should celebrate without understanding what we celebrate,
or, like our counterparts so long ago, fail to see the star or to hear the song of glorious promise.

As our hearts yield to the spirit of Christmas, may we discover that it is Thy Holy Spirit who comes—not a sentiment, but a power—to remind us of the only way by which there may be peace on the earth and good will among men.

May we not spend Christmas, but keep it, that we may be kept in its hope, through Him who emptied Himself in coming to us that we might be filled with peace and joy in returning to God.
Amen.

PETER MARSHALL

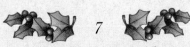

May You Know Joy

May you, wherever you are in
this golden hour, know joy.
May your hearth fire be surrounded
with those near and dear to you;
and may the happiness of your children
Re-echo the gladness heaven sends forth
in this time of the miracle of Bethlehem.

May the faith the humble shepherds
found in the starlit stable
be yours in fullest measure;
and may the exultation of Mary and Joseph
light your heart with the glow of divine love.

May you gather together in bright bouquet
love, charity, and tranquility of spirit;
for he who possesses these holds
the key to riches beyond measure.

May all your dreams in this splendid hour
reach fulfillment; and may all the paths you walk
be lighted with peace, not only today,
but in all the days of the year to come.

LORETTA BAUER BUCKLEY

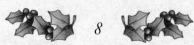

9

Christmas Families

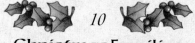

Christmas Families

O Simplicitas

An angel came to me
And I was unprepared
To be what God was using.
Mother I was to be.
A moment I despaired,
Thought briefly of refusing.
The angel knew I heard.
According to God's Word
I bowed to this strange choosing.

A palace should have been
The birthplace of a king
(I had no way of knowing).
We went to Bethlehem;
It was so strange a thing.
The wind was cold, and blowing,
My cloak was old, and thin.
They turned us from the inn;
The town was overflowing.

God's Word, a child so small,
Who still must learn to speak,
Lay in humiliation.
Joseph stood, strong and tall.
The beasts were warm and meek
And moved with hesitation.
The Child born in a stall?
I understood it: all.
Kings came in adoration.

Perhaps it was absurd:
The stable set apart,
The sleepy cattle lowing;
And the incarnate Word
Resting against my heart.
My joy was overflowing.
The shepherds came, adored
The folly of the Lord,
Wiser than all men's knowing.

MADELEINE L'ENGLE

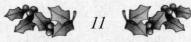

11

Christmas Families

A Cradle Song

Sweet dreams, form a shade
O'er my lovely infant's head;
Sweet dreams of pleasant streams
By happy, silent, moony beams.

Sweet sleep, with soft down
Weave thy brows an infant crown.
Sweet sleep, angel mild,
Hover o'er my happy child.

Sweet smiles, in the night
Hover over my delight;
Sweet smiles, mother's smiles,
All the livelong night beguiles.

Sweet moans, dovelike sighs,
Chase not slumber from thy eyes.
Sweet moans, sweeter smiles,
All the dovelike moans beguiles.

Sleep, sleep, happy child,
All creation slept and smil'd;
Sleep, sleep, happy sleep,
While o'er thee thy mother weep.

Sweet babe, in thy face
Holy image I can trace.
Sweet babe once like thee,
Thy Maker lay and wept for me,

Wept for me, for thee, for all,
When He was an infant small.
Thou His image ever see,
Heavenly face that smiles on thee,

Smiles on thee, on me, on all;
Who became an infant small.
Infant smiles are His own smiles;
Heaven and earth to peace beguiles.

WILLIAM BLAKE

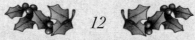

Christmas Families

Christmas Families

Joseph

How weary and how tired
they must have been,
Coming from Nazareth
since the day's pale start,
Joseph with great responsibility,
Mary bearing earth's Saviour 'neath her heart.
Nearing the village at the set of the sun,
The man must hasten for a place to rest;
He watched the woman with grave, anxious eyes,
Seeing her clutch a white hand to her breast.

Was she too tired? Had they come too far?
Had his love failed this gentle, precious one?
And now the crowded inn, the words "No room"
For Mary soon to mother God's dear Son!
Joseph was deeply troubled. Could there be
No place in all this throng for them to go?
Then, suddenly, the stable and a hand
Bidding them enter. God had planned it so!

GRACE NOLL CROWELL

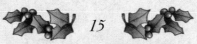

I Do Not Ask of Thee

Dear Lord, I do not ask of Thee
Always to smooth the path for me,
But grant me strength enough to bear
Whate'er my portion is of care.
Now for my children's sake, I pray,
Help me to walk in wisdom's way.

Let me not blunder. To the end
Their happiness I would defend.
Grant me to earn their gratitude,
To understand their every mood,
And through the labyrinth of youth
Guide them to everlasting truth.

Dear Lord, I pray Thee, make of me
The father Thou wouldst have me be.
Let me not hastily condemn
Or ever ask too much of them,
And when their little feet have strayed,
Of me let them be unafraid.

God grant me this, all else above,
That I may keep my children's love
And lead them on to all that's good
Of manhood and of womanhood;
That I, when childhood's years have flown,
In their success may find my own.

EDGAR A. GUEST

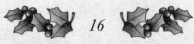

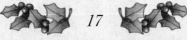

Christmas Families

Lord Jesus, You Who Bade the Children Come

Lord Jesus, You who bade
the children come
And took them in
Your gentle arms and smiled,
Grant me the unfailing patience through the days
To understand and help my little child.

I would not only give his body care
And guide his young dependent steps along
The wholesome ways, but I would know his heart,
Attuning mine to childhood's griefs and song.

Oh, give me vision to discern the child
Behind whatever he may do or say,
The wise humility to learn from him
The while I strive to teach him day by day.

ADELAIDE LOVE

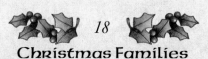

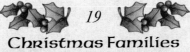

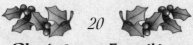

There Will Be Christmas

As long as there are homes
where families meet
And pray a little prayer
before they eat;
As long as there are homes
where children play
And echo forth their joy
in childlike way;
As long as there are homes
where parents care
And teach their children often
how to share;
As long as there are homes
with candle glow
That sends a shining beacon
o'er the snow;
As long as there are homes
built fast on love;
As long as there are those
who look above;
As long as there are homes
who let Christ in,
Who hear Him, heed Him, hold Him
through the earth's great din—
There will be Christmas!

ESTHER L. DAUBER

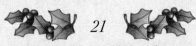

For Our Children

Father, hear us, we are praying,
Hear the words our hearts are saying,
We are praying for our children.

Keep them from the powers of evil,
From the secret, hidden peril,
From the whirlpool that would suck them,
From the treacherous quicksand, pluck them.

From the worldling's hollow gladness,
From the sting of faithless sadness,
Holy Father, save our children.

Through life's troubled waters steer them,
Through life's bitter battle cheer them,
Father, Father, be Thou near them.
Read the language of our longing,
Read the wordless pleadings thronging,
Holy Father, for our children.

And wherever they may bide,
Lead them Home at eventide.

AMY CARMICHAEL

23

Christmas Families

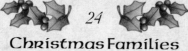 24

Christmas Families

Almighty God, Heavenly Father

Almighty God, heavenly Father,
who seest our families
and the homes in
which they dwell:
Deliver us, we beseech
Thee, from vainglory,
selfish pride,
and every cause of bitterness.
Endue us with faith, temperance,
and patience.
Knit together in true affection
those who in holy wedlock have
been made one flesh.
Turn the heart of the parents
to their children
and the heart of the children
to their parents,
in mutual respect and love,
and make us kindly affectioned
to one another
in the spirit of Thy blessed Son,
our Saviour, Jesus Christ.

THE BOOK OF COMMON PRAYER

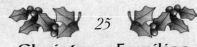

A Christmas Tree Prayer

Lord, bless the hands
that made this tree
Such a lovely thing to see,
And oh, dear Lord,
we pray that Thou
Will bless each special little bough.

The white dove rests here from its flight
In search of peace on earth tonight.
On wings of love may it then find
Brotherhood for all mankind.

Oh, may the gleam of tinseled rope
Renew our faith, rebuild our hope;
And may the star atop the tree
Lead us always nearer Thee.

LAURA BAKER HAYNES

O Heavenly Father

O heavenly Father, who long ago
didst watch Thy son on earth grow
as in stature so in wisdom
and in perfect love of Thee:
teach by the wondrous life of Jesus
and His church the children
whom Thou watchest now;
that they may grow into His likeness,
loving Thee, obedient to Thy will,
and happy in Thy house;
through the same Jesus Christ our Lord.
Amen.

THE BOOK OF COMMON PRAYER

Not What I Hold

I hold in my hands some elflike things—
A new toy soldier; gossamered wings
From a Christmas angel; boughs of green;
Red ribbons tied to a tambourine;
Glistening trimmings, chic, debonair;
Ornaments bright with a holiday flair.
Strange I should hold to the tinseled part
When not in my hands but in my heart
Are all the best of my treasures stored—
Love, and each other, the Christ adored.
The greatest of these will ever be
Not that which I hold but what holds me.

WILLIAM TRALL DONCASTER, JR.

The Day after Christmas

O Lord Jesus, we thank Thee
for the joys of this season,
for the divine love that was shed
abroad among men when
Thou didst first come as a little child.

But may we not think of Thy coming
as a distant event that took place once
and has never been repeated.
May we know that Thou art still here
walking among us, by our sides,
whispering over our shoulders,
tugging at our sleeves,
smiling upon us when we need
encouragement and help.

We thank Thee for Thy spirit
that moves at this season the hearts of men:
to be kindly and thoughtful—where before
they were careless and indifferent;
to be generous—where before
they lived in selfishness;

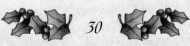

to be gentle—where before they had been
rough and unmindful of the weak;
to express their love—where before it had
been taken for granted and assumed.

We are learning—O Lord, so slowly—
life's true values. Surely Christmas would
teach us the unforgettable lesson
of the things that matter most—
the ties that bind the structure
of the family upon which our country
and all the world rests; the love that
we have for one another which binds
Thy whole creation to Thy footstool,
Thy throne. We are learning slowly,
but, O God, we thank Thee
that we are learning.

So may Christmas linger with us,
even as Thou art beside us
the whole year through.
Amen.

PETER MARSHALL

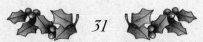

Christmas Blessings

And Joseph also went up from Galilee, out of the city of Nazareth, into Judœa, unto the city of David, which is called Bethlehem: ... To be taxed with Mary his espoused wife, being great with child. And so it was, that, while they were there, the days were accomplished that she should be delivered. And she brought forth her firstborn son, and wrapped him in swaddling clothes, and laid him in a manger; because there was no room for them in the inn.

LUKE 2:4-7

Christmas Prayer

May Christmas come to bless you
On its gentle wings of love
With moments sweet and tender,
With God's blessings from above.
May a smile and breath of kindness,
A warm hand that grasps your own
Weave a day of deeper meaning
And dearer worth into your home.

May Christmas come to bless you
On its joyous wings of song.
When voices of the angels
All are singing clear and strong,
May the bell high in the steeple
Peal its message through the sky;
May you hear the song of heaven
Softly bid your heart reply.

May Christmas come to bless you
On its holy wings of peace
When your quiet mind is richer
And your soul finds sweet release.
May you know love's warm bestowing
And the joy that fills the air;
And may you, like little children,
Reach for Him on wings of prayer.

JOY BELLE BURGESS

Make Me a Blessing

ake me a blessing, Lord! Help me
To help those needing help, to be
A blessing to my fellowmen.
Instruct me when to speak and when
To hold my speech, when to be bold
In giving and when to withhold;
And if I have not strength enough,
Then give me strength. Lord, make me love
Myself and tender be toward
All others. Let there be outpoured
On me the gentleness to bless
All who have need of gentleness.
Give me a word, a touch to fill
The lonely life, faith for the ill,
And courage to keep hearts up though
My own is feeling just as low.
When men have bitter things to meet
And quail and would accept defeat,
Then let me lift their eyes to see
The vision of Thy victory.
Help me to help; help me to give
The wisdom and the will to live.

JAMES DILLET FREEMAN

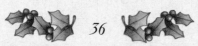

Christmas Blessings

Christmas Blessings

One Small Child

One little child . . . no more, no less—
And could His mother Mary guess
Salvation for the human race
Depended on that night, that place?
And did she know this child would cause
All heaven to rock with glad applause?

Would cause the angels to rehearse
Their midnight song of sacred verse?
Would cause a star of strange design
To leave its orbit, and to shine

A brilliant path, from east to west?
Would cause the wise men to choose the best
Of hoarded treasure, and to search
The nations from a camel perch?

Would make a king (in craven fear)
Destroy small man-children near?
To this small child the nation thrilled,
For He was prophecy fulfilled.

But could His mother, even, guess
While rocking Him with tenderness
The whole import of His advent,
This one small child—from heaven sent.

ESTHER S. BUCKWALTER

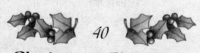

Ponderings

Did she, His mother, reminisce,
And did it go a bit like this?
"Just as my time was 'bout to be,
My husband said by some decree
We had to go, so he'd been told,
To Bethlehem to be enrolled.
It was a dirty, weary ride,
And Joseph walked it by my side.
When we arrived among his kin,
There was no lodging at the inn.
But in compassion someone gave
Directions to a little cave,
And in that shelter so forlorn
My little baby boy was born.

So sweet and gentle right from birth!
And yet I knew He'd change the earth.
I had been told He was God's Son,
And, as His life was just begun,
Above us shone a holy star
That drew three wise men from afar.
From hills nearby the shepherds came
And called my baby by His name.
They said that angels had appeared
And calmed the ones who plainly feared
By telling them of peace, good will:
A prophecy that He'd fulfill.
All this had set my child apart.
These things I've pondered in my heart."

MARGARET RORKE

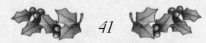

A Christmas Prayer

O God our loving Father, help us rightly to remember the birth of Jesus, that we may share in the song of the angels, the gladness of the shepherds, and the worship of the wise men.

Close the door of hate, and open the door of love all over the world.

Deliver us from evil by the blessing that Christ brings, and teach us to be merry with clear hearts.

May the Christmas morning make us happy to be Thy children and the Christmas evening bring us to our beds with grateful thoughts, forgiving and forgiven, for Jesus' sake.
Amen.

ROBERT LOUIS STEVENSON

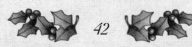

Christmas Blessings

A Christmas Wish

 wish you joy on Christmas Day.
Yet one day filled
with mirth and cheer
Will oh so quickly pass away;
I wish you joy throughout the year.

May peace be yours
when night comes down;
May every good which life can give
Be yours to bless your home and crown
The tasks of every day you live.

Beneath your roof may laughter ring
And love and merriment abide,
And may you reap through many a spring
The blossoms of the countryside.

God grant that you may wake by day
In strength, the tasks of life to meet;
May you go singing down the way,
And may your dreams at night be sweet.

Through every day of every year
This wish of mine I shall renew;
God keep you safe and hold you dear
And pour His blessings down on you.

EDGAR A. GUEST

Hay, Did You Say?

Hay! Hay, did you say?
Surely it was not hay
On which the Christ Child lay?
Humble indeed the shed,
Awkward the manger bed,
Was there no linen spread?
Come, was it hay you said?

Yes, it was common hay,
Cut on a summer's day.
As the sweet crop they drest—
Dividing the good from best—
They knew not some would rest
This world's most holy guest.

AUTHOR UNKNOWN

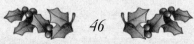

Christmas Blessings

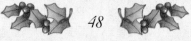 48

Christmas Blessings

A Season Blest

Give us, O Lord, a season blest
With quiet joys for Thy domain:
Let kindness calm the earth's unrest
And bring a peace to rough terrain.
Dispose of monetary powers
On land prolific with Thy seeds;
Bestow within the Yuletide hours
A unity of manmade creeds.

Like rain that permeates and soothes
Dry plains, saturate the nations.
Return the world to simple truths
Taught wisely by Thy Son of sons.

We hunger for Thee in our strife,
Become again the bread of life.

BETTY GARDNER ACKERLIND

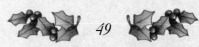

A Christmas Carol

God bless you all this Christmas Day
And drive the cares and griefs away.
Oh, may the shining Bethlehem star
Which leads the wise men from afar
Upon your heads, good sirs, still glow
To light the path that you should go.

As God once blessed the stable grim
And made it radiant for Him,
As it was fit to shield His Son,
May thy roof be a holy one.
May all who come this house to share
Rest sweetly in His gracious care.

Within thy walls may peace abide—
The peace for which the Saviour died.
Though humble be the rafters here,
Above them may the stars shine clear,
And in this home thou lovest well
May excellence of spirit dwell.

God bless you all this Christmas Day.
May Bethlehem's star still light the way
And guide thee to the perfect peace
When every fear and doubt shall cease.
And may thy home such glory know
As did the stable long ago.

EDGAR A. GUEST

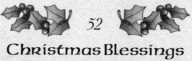 52

Christmas Blessings

For Christmas the Year Round

 come to my heart, Lord Jesus;
there is room in my heart for Thee."

Lord Jesus, we thank Thee for
the spirit shed abroad in human hearts
on Christmas. Even as we invited Thee
on Christmas to be born again in our hearts,
so wilt Thou now go with us throughout
the days ahead, to be our companion
in all that we do. Wilt Thou help each one of us
to keep Christmas alive in our hearts
and in our homes, that it may continue to glow,
to shed its warmth, to speak its message
during all the bleak days of winter.

May we hold to that spirit, that we may be
as gentle and as kindly today
as we were on Christmas Eve,
as generous tomorrow
as we were on Christmas morning.

Then if—by Thy help—we should live through
a whole week in that spirit, it may be we can
go into another week, and thus be encouraged
and gladdened by the discovery that Christmas
can last the year round.

So give us joyful, cheerful hearts
to the glory of Jesus Christ, our Lord.
Amen.

PETER MARSHALL

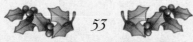

Christmas Faith

And there were in the same country shepherds abiding in the field, keeping watch over their flock by night. And, lo, the angel of the Lord came upon them, and the glory of the Lord shone round about them: and they were sore afraid. And the angel said unto them, Fear not: for, behold, I bring you good tidings of great joy, which shall be to all people. For unto you is born this day in the city of David a Saviour, which is Christ the Lord. And this shall be a sign unto you; Ye shall find the babe wrapped in swaddling clothes, lying in a manger.

LUKE 2:8-12

Lord, Increase Our Faith

Lord, increase our faith.
We believe; help Thou
our unbelief. Give us a true
child's trust in Thee,
in all Thy strength and goodness.
Cause us to rest in perfect confidence
in all Thy purposes and ways.
Enable us to confide
all our interests for time
and for eternity to Thy keeping.
Give us, heavenly Father,
the substance of things hoped for
and the evidence of things unseen,
that we may walk by faith, not by sight,
looking not at the things
which are seen and temporal
but at those things
which are not seen and eternal.

AUTHOR UNKNOWN

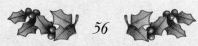

Christmas Faith

Later Christmas Eves

n after years when
angels came no longer,
When skies were mute
for all your grief and loss,
In after years on Christmas Eve, O Mary,
Which filled your heart—the manger or the cross?

I shall believe your Son looked down in pity
To lift the ache which you had borne so long,
And on the eve bid you remember only
The child within your arms, the star, the song.

I shall believe that Joseph came to find you,
Returning from some neighbor shepherd's fold,
And laid within your arms a lamb to fondle,
And spoke your name, and knelt as once of old.

ADELAIDE LOVE

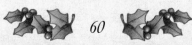

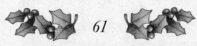
Christmas Faith

Winter

As the snow falls gently
against my window, I give thanks,
O divine Spirit, for the cycle
of the seasons and the ever-changing
beauty of the universe.
A mantle of purity is spread over this drab earth,
and the evergreens bow humbly
in their vestments of white. The noises
of men cease; a new stillness envelopes
the world, and Thy voice speaks to me
through the elements.

Surely the power that can create
a billion snowflakes, in numberless variety
and of perfect symmetrical form
to sparkle for a moment in the sunlight
and then vanish, is also mindful of me
and the length of my days.

As I look upon this beauty, I think
of Thee as the source from which it all comes,
and I am drawn closer to Thee.
Give me faith to believe that the order
which sustains the ever-varying pageantry
of nature will also uphold me.
Lord of life, make me quiet long enough
to hear Thee speak above the murmur
of my desires, the clamor of much speaking,
and the confusions of mankind.
Breathe into my life the peace
and purity of the snow.
Amen.

ROBERT MERRILL BARTLETT

Give Us, O Lord, a Steadfast Heart

Give us, O Lord, a steadfast heart,
which no unworthy
affection may drag down;
give us an unconquered heart,
which no tribulation can wear out;
give us an upright heart,
which no unworthy purpose may tempt aside.
Bestow upon us also, O Lord our God,
understanding to know Thee,
diligence to seek Thee,
wisdom to find Thee,
and a faithfulness that may
finally embrace Thee,
even through Jesus Christ our Lord.

THOMAS AQUINAS

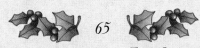

The Inn:
The Landlord Speaks A.D. 28

What could be done? The inn was full of folks!
His honor, Marcus Lucius, and his scribes
Who made the census: honorable men
From farthest Galilee, come hitherward
To be enrolled; high ladies and their lords;
The rich, the rabbis, such a noble throng
As Bethlehem had never seen before
And may not see again. And there they were,
Close-herded with their servants, till the inn
Was like a hive at swarming-time, and I
Was fairly crazed among them.

Could I know
That they were so important? Just the two,
No servants, just a workman sort of man,
Leading a donkey, and his wife thereon
Drooping and pale . . . I saw them not myself;
My servants must have driven them away.
But had I seen them, how was I to know?
Were inns to welcome stragglers, up and down
In all our towns from Beersheba to Dan,
Till He should come? And how were men to know?

There was a sign, they say, a heavenly light
Resplendent; but I had not time for stars.

And there were songs of angels in the air
Out on the hills, but how was I to hear
Amid the thousand clamors of an inn?
Of course, if I had known them, who they were,
And who was He that should be born that night,
For now I learn that they will make Him king,
A second David, who will ransom us
From these Philistine Romans . . . who but He
That feeds an army with a loaf of bread,
And if a soldier falls, He touches him
And up he leaps, uninjured? Had I known,
I would have turned the whole inn upside down—
His honor, Marcus Lucius, and the rest—
And sent them all to stables, had I known.

So you have seen Him, stranger, and perhaps
Again may see Him? Prithee say for me,
I did not know; and if He comes again
As He will surely come, with retinue,
And banners, and an army, tell my Lord
That all my inn is His to make amends.

Alas! Alas! To miss a chance like that!
This inn that might be chief among them all,
The birthplace of Messiah . . . had I known!

AMOS RUSSELL WELLS

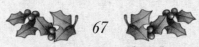

Winter

When my leaves fall,
wilt Thou encompass them?
The gold of autumn flown,
the bare branch brown,
The brittle twig and stem,
The tired leaves dropping down,
Wilt thou encompass that which men call dead?
I see the rain, the coldly smothering snow,
My leaves dispirited,
Lie very low.

So the heart questioneth, white Winter near;
Till jocund as the glorious voice of Spring
Cometh his, "Do not fear,
But sing, rejoice and sing,
For sheltered by the coverlet of snow
Are secrets of delight, and there shall be
Uprising that shall show
All that through winter I prepared for thee."

AMY CARMICHAEL

Christmas Faith

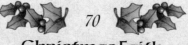

Christmas Faith

A Prayer

Thou art not far from any one of us,
However far we are, O Lord, from Thee.
Give us the grace of quietness to know
Thy presence and Thy holy harmony
Within our hearts through all the hurried hours,
Through all the clamorous din of busy days,
Till in the listening silence of our souls
There stirs a song of worship and praise,
A song of praise to Thee for all Thy love,
A song of love for every living thing
That Thou, our Father and our God, hast made.
Oh, teach us to be still, that we may sing.

JANE MERCHANT

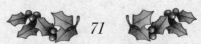

Lead, Kindly Light

Lead, kindly Light,
amid the encircling gloom,
Lead Thou me on!
The night is dark
and I am far from home—
Lead Thou me on!
Keep Thou my feet; I do not ask to see
The distant scene—one step enough for me.

I was not ever thus, nor prayed that
Thou Shouldst lead me on.
I loved to choose and see my path; but now
Lead Thou me on!
I loved the garish day, and, spite of fears,
Pride ruled my will:
Remember not past years.

So long Thy power has blest me, sure it still
Will lead me on
O'er moor and fen, o'er crag and torrent, till
The night is gone;
And with the morn those angel faces smile
Which I have loved long since,
And lost awhile!

JOHN HENRY NEWMAN

For a Renaissance of Faith

Our Father, remove from us
the sophistication of our age
and the skepticism that has come,
like frost, to blight our faith
and to make it weak.
Bring us back to a faith that
makes men great and strong,
a faith that enables us to love and to live,
the faith by which we are triumphant,
the faith by which alone
we can walk with Thee.

We pray for a return of that simple faith,
that old-fashioned trust in God,
that made strong and great the homes
of our ancestors who built this good land
and who in building left us our heritage.
In the strong name of Jesus, our Lord,
we make this prayer.

PETER MARSHALL

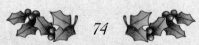

Christmas Faith

Christmas Journeys

Then Herod, when he had privily called the wise men, enquired of them diligently what time the star appeared. And he sent them to Bethlehem, and said, Go and search diligently for the young child; ... When they had heard the king, they departed; and, lo, the star, which they saw in the east, went before them, till it came and stood over where the young child was. When they saw the star, they rejoiced with exceeding great joy.

MATTHEW 2:7-10

The Road
to Christmas

For this clear, starry
night let us forget
The clamor of the world,
our doubts, our fears,
The threatening war clouds
red against the East,
And let us take the road
back through the years:
A road, alas, forgotten all too long,
A road from which
mankind has wandered far,
The only road miraculously lit
By the hand of God with an eternal star.

And if we travel facing toward the sky,
That star will send a silver radiance down
To light the way for all who strive to reach
The Christ Child, cradled in a darkened town:
The Saviour come to ease our troubled minds,
To point out pathways that we do not know,
To illuminate the darkest, deepest night.
O hearts, He is waiting for us, let us go!

GRACE NOLL CROWELL

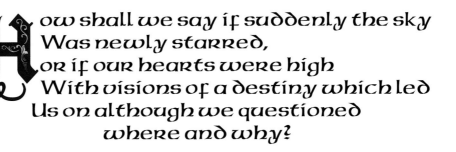

The Wise Men's Story

How shall we say if suddenly the sky
  Was newly starred,
Or if our hearts were high
  With visions of a destiny which led
Us on although we questioned
  where and why?

We followed love, and we were comforted
On that long journey by a light which fed
Our souls with faith which did not fade or die,
A light whose source lay on a manger bed.

We hoped to find a child but did not know
He would be in a stable, poor and small,
But filled with joy so great it seemed to flow
Like music, making every dream grow tall.

We are three kings who sought a palace door
But knelt, instead, to worship on a stable floor.

LOLA S. MORGAN

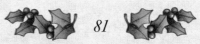

A Christmas Prayer

The road to ancient Bethlehem
Leads out too endlessly,
But at my window I can kneel,
Dear Lord, to worship Thee.
I see through the bright silver mist
Of starlight down my street
The startled shepherds moving out
On eager, hurrying feet
To fall before Thee, blessed Lord.
I see the wise men ride
High on their rocking beasts to come
And worship at Thy side.
I cannot join the throngs tonight
To journey to Thy stall,
But Lord, dear Lord, I bring my gifts:
My love, my life, my all.

GRACE NOLL CROWELL

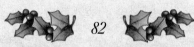

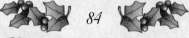

Christmas Journeys

The Christmas Hope

The star that shone in Bethlehem
In that resplendent year
Brought cheer and comfort
to men's hearts
And cast out doubt and fear.
The wise men left their eastern homes
And came through deserts wild
To lay their treasures at the feet
Of Christ, God's holy Child.

Alas, for angels' song of peace!
Alas, for wise men's dreams!
And yet, and yet that hope still lives;
Still shines that bright star's gleam.
God's will still stands; faith is not dead:
Men yet should hail the day
When Christ shall take his long-lost throne
And love shall light the way.

THOMAS CURTIS CLARK

A Christmas Dream

I heard the bells
of Christmastide
In the hush before the morn,
Telling again the promise true
That Christ the king was born.

I walked the hills of Bethlehem
And heard the angels sing,
As shepherds watched
their flocks by night,
"Hosannas to the King!"

I saw the bright and shining star
That guided the wise men three
To the little town of Bethlehem
Where the holy babe would be.

I trod the streets of Bethlehem,
Found the lowly stable where
The Christ Child in the manger laid,
And dropped to my knees in prayer.

Yes, I heard the bells of Christmas ring
In the silence before the morn—
Rekindling in the hearts of man
The miracle of Christ newborn.

FLORENCE HOWERY RODDY

At This Time of Year

At this time of year,
the church bells pealing softly
in the distance remind us that
we need to journey again, in spirit,
to Bethlehem. Down a narrow, cobbled street
we thread our way to a crude stable
where we find the Saviour
wrapped in swaddling clothes.
Though of humble lineage,
He is the Christ, the King of kings,
the Prince of peace,
the true meaning of Christmas.

And, with reflection upon a world
fraught with crises and tumult,
we pause there to give
thanks to God for His Son,
for liberty, and for life itself.

May the true meaning of Christmas
abide with you and yours this day.

GEORGIA B. ADAMS

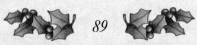

Moonless Darkness

Moonless darkness
stands between.
Past, O Past,
no more be seen!
But the Bethlehem star
may lead me
To the sight of Him
who freed me
From the self that I have been.

Make me pure, Lord:
Thou art holy;
Make me meek, Lord:
Thou wert lowly;
Now beginning, and always:
Now begin, on Christmas Day.

GERARD MANLEY HOPKINS

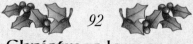

Christmas: Another Way

When wise men found the Saviour Child
That wondrous, far-off Christmas Day,
They journeyed homeward once again
But traveled back Another Way.

For them, and us, Another Way
To follow in the search for truth,
To learn the wisdom of this world
That lights the minds of age and youth.

Another way of love to God,
And saving love for all mankind,
The way of faith and light and hope
The ancient world could never find.

Another way to live and serve,
Designed to meet our brothers' needs,
To show compassion and uplift
With healing words and loving deeds.

Another Way of Christ-like love
Would turn our weary world around,
If men would go to Bethlehem
And find what questing wise men found.

J. HAROLD GWYNNE

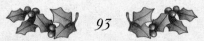

The Returning Christ

At Christmastime when every heart
With special rapture fills,
Each soul becomes a Bethlehem
Among Judean hills,

And Jesus Christ, the Son of God,
In His own lowly way,
Comes seeking room in human hearts
To share the Christmas Day.

May He not find the crowded inn
Too full for Him again,
Or Christmas gifts and Christmas trees
Without the Christ of men.

But may there be the humble heart
With room prepared and blessed,
And hearts reborn to greet anew
The long-expected guest.

At Christmas when He seeks His place
Supreme in human wills,
Each heart becomes a Bethlehem
Among Judean hills.

BETTY W. STOFFEL

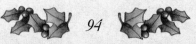

Christmas Journeys

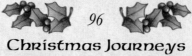 96

Guide Our Steps

Guide our steps, O Lord,
this Christmastide
Along the path which
Thou hast trod
That we may draw nearer
here on earth
To the brotherhood of man
Beneath the fatherhood of God.

Bless our lives, O Lord,
the new year through
That in each act we may fulfill
The commandment of love
our Christ defined,
Which will bring a peace on earth
To men who demonstrate good will.

KATHY MATTHEWS

Christmas Gifts

And when they were come into the house, they saw the young child with Mary his mother, and fell down, and worshipped him: and when they had opened their treasures, they presented unto him gifts; gold, and frankincense, and myrrh. And being warned of God in a dream that they should not return to Herod, they departed into their own country another way.

MATTHEW 2:11-12

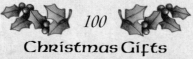

By the Shining of a Star

O God, who by the shining of a star didst guide the wise men to behold Thy Son our Lord, show us Thy heavenly light, and give us grace to follow until we find Him, and, finding Him, rejoice.

And grant that as they presented gold, frankincense, and myrrh, we now may bring Him the offering of a loving heart, an adoring spirit, and an obedient will, for His honor, and for Thy glory, O God Most High. Amen.

BOOK OF COMMON WORSHIP

Christmas Gifts

The Gift

The shepherd boy pondered,
"What can I bring?
What does a shepherd boy
Give to a king?

If I were a rich man,
I would bring Him gold;
If I were a wise man,
Tales untold.

But I'm just a shepherd boy
Tending my sheep;
High on a hillside
My watch I keep."

Then the voices of angels
Called from above,
"Good little shepherd boy,
Just bring Him your love."

NANCY L. KRATOWICZ

Lord, Bless the Cards We've Written

Lord, bless the cards we've written;
May they bear a joyous greeting.
Bless the gifts we've wrapped and tied;
May they radiate Thy love.
Bless the wreaths that we have hung
In doorway, stair, and hall;
May they speak of life eternal,
Thy dominion over all.

Bless the lovely candle
Shining forth into the night;
May it carry far and wide
The wondrous message of Thy light.
Bless all the sweet traditions of
Thy dear, holy birth;
May they lead us in the worship of
The Saviour, Lord of Earth.

MYRTLE BEELER DAY

 *105*

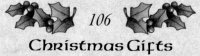

Let This Be Borne in Every Heart

On that first Christmas night of all
(Let this be borne in every heart),
The simple beasts of fold and stall
Had each its quiet part.

When music broke above the hill
And all the shepherds swift were gone,
In patience through the dark and chill
The lonely flocks stayed on.

Down at the stable, ox and ass
Stood close together in the gloom,
Not knowing who this stranger was
But fain to give Him room.

The Lord of all remembers them;
On humble back and gentle head,
Each Christmastime, the light is shed
That shone in Bethlehem.

NANCY BYRD TURNER

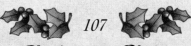

We Thank Thee, Heavenly Father

We thank Thee, heavenly Father,
for the swift, pure loveliness
of falling snow that makes us
young again with wonder and delight.
We thank Thee for all the myriad
unexpected ways in which
Thou dost surprise our eyes with beauty
so that we forget for a moment
our small preoccupations,
exulting in the works
that Thou hast wrought.
In Christ's name,
Amen.

JANE MERCHANT

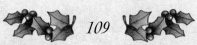

To His Saviour, a Child:
A Present by a Child

Go, pretty child, and bear this flower
 Unto thy little Saviour;
And tell Him, by that bud now blown,
 He is the Rose of Sharon known.
When thou hast said so, stick it there
 Upon His bib or stomacher;
And tell Him, for good handsel, too,
That thou hast brought a whistle new,
 Made of clean strait oaken reed,
To charm His cries at time of need.
Tell Him, for coral, thou hast none,
But if thou hadst, he should have one;
But poor thou art, and known to be
 Even as moneyless as He.
Lastly, if thou canst win a kiss
From those mellifluous lips of His;
Then never take a second on,
To spoil the first impression.

ROBERT HERRICK

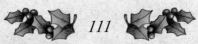

Christmas Gifts

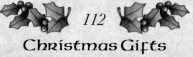

Christmas Gifts

Gifts of Love

For us Christ gave His all in all;
He died that we might live;
And so our mission here should be
To love, to help, to give.

A million gifts could not repay
The one of love divine;
And yet if true love prompts each gift,
Our gifts will count, in time.

So give, not hoping to receive
Like gifts from friend or kin,
But with a motive greater far—
The heartfelt love within.

Remember then this Christmastime
The needy and the troubled,
And share the blessings you receive—
You'll find your joy has doubled.

ANNA B. SMITH

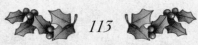

A Christmas Blessing

ay the light of His love
And the glow of His star
Spread the brightness
of Christmas
Wherever you are
And the songs of the angels
Who once hovered near
Tune your spirit to music
While Christmas is here.

May the joy of His presence
Be with you today—
A treasure unending,
Not passing away—
While the peace of the season
Awaiting each heart
That turns to the manger
Be yours from the start.

The gifts wrapped in tissue
Forgotten will be
In the years just ahead,
Great or small though they be;
But the gift God has given
From heaven above
In the form of our Saviour
Is unfading love.

LOUISE WEIBERT SUTTON

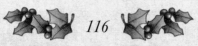

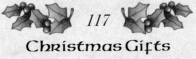

Christmas Gifts

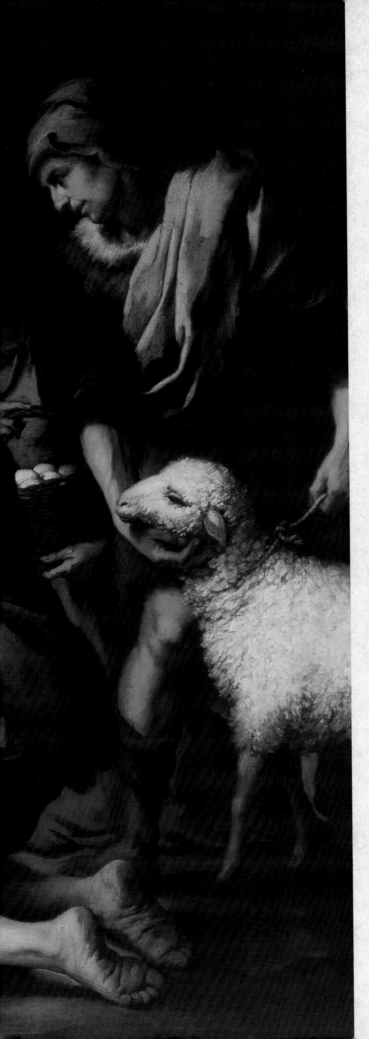

Christmas Adoration

And suddenly there was with the angel a multitude of the heavenly host praising God, and saying, Glory to God in the highest, and on earth peace, good will toward men. And it came to pass, as the angels were gone away from them into heaven, the shepherds said one to another, Let us now go even unto Bethlehem, and see this thing which is come to pass, which the Lord hath made known unto us.

LUKE 2:13-15

I Must Never Lose the Wonder

I must never lose the wonder
Of that first glad Christmas night
When the star high in the heavens
Lent its pure and holy light.

I must trace again the footsteps
To the stable, bleak and bare,
Where my Saviour lies asleeping
In the humble manger there.

I must blend my voice with angels
As they sing their song on high,
As they stretch their giant wingspans
Out across the velvet sky.

I must gather with the shepherds
And the wise men from afar;
I must never lose the wonder,
The sheer wonder, of this hour!

GEORGIA B. ADAMS

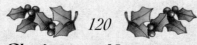

On This Hallowed Eve of Christmas

On this hallowed eve of Christmas
may you discover anew
the splendor of the star,
the exultant song of herald angels,
the immeasurable love of Mary and Joseph.

May you find in the child of the manger
all that you seek:
faith, hope, a deeper understanding
of charity and brotherly love.

In this golden hour
of the miracle of Bethlehem
may the beauty of quiet thoughts
encompass your heart,
the tenderness of the mother's smile,
the adoration of humble shepherds.

With the brilliancy of the star
may the year that lies ahead
be lighted, the days as a jeweled
chain kept ever lustrous
with the divine love
for which the Prince of peace
was born into the world.

LORETTA BAUER BUCKLEY

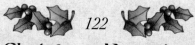

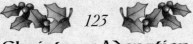 *123*

Christmas Adoration

Paradox

Here lies the precious babe,
First-fruit of virgin's womb,
Angels' delight and joy,
Men's highest price and boon,
Should He your Saviour be
And lift you into God,
Then, man, stay near the crib
And make it your abode.

How simple we must grow!
How simple they, who came!
The shepherds looked at God
Long before any man.
He sees God nevermore
Not there, nor here on earth
Who does not long within
To be a shepherd first.

All things are now reversed:
The castle's in the cave,
The crib becomes the throne,
The night brings forth the day,
The virgin bears a child.
O man! Reflect and say
That heart and mind must be
Reversed in every way.

ANGELUS SILESIUS

Christmas Adoration

Christmas Praise

Praise to God this Christmas night
For the star that beams on high,
For the angel voices clear,
For their song that fills the sky.
Sing with saints and angels bright:
"Praise to God this Christmas night!"

Thanks to God this Christmas Day
For His grace and endless love,
For the gift of Christ, His Son,
Come to earth from heaven above.
With the saints and angels say:
"Thanks to God this Christmas Day!"

Lift your hearts in prayer this day.
Pray the Christ Child come within,
That He end the night of sin,
That the reign of peace begin.
As we seek His holy way,
Let us pray this Christmas Day.

Sing we then the joyous song:
"Christ the Lord is born this night!"
May your heart receive Him now,
With His peace, His joy, His light.
Sing with saints and angels bright:
"Christ the Lord is born this night!"

ANNA D. LUTZ

Ring Out, Wild Bells

Ring out, wild bells, to the wild sky,
The flying cloud, the frosty light:
The year is dying in the night;
Ring out, wild bells, and let him die.

Ring out the old, ring in the new,
Ring happy bells across the snow:
The year is going, let him go;
Ring out the false, ring in the true.

Ring out the grief that saps the mind,
For those that here we see no more;
Ring out the feud of rich and poor,
Ring in redress to all mankind.

Ring out a slowly dying cause
And ancient forms of party strife;
Ring in the nobler forms of life
With sweeter manners, purer laws.

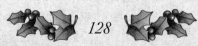

Ring out the want, the care, the sin,
The faithless coldness of the times;
Ring out, ring out my mournful rhymes,
But ring the fuller minstrel in.

Ring out false pride in place and blood,
The civic slander and the spite;
Ring in the love of truth and right;
Ring in the common love of good.

Ring out old shapes of foreign disease;
Ring out the narrowing lust of gold;
Ring out the thousand wars of old;
Ring in the thousand years of peace.

Ring in the valiant man and free,
The larger heart, the kindlier hand;
Ring out the darkness of the land;
Ring in the Christ that is to be.

ALFRED, LORD TENNYSON

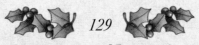

A Little Child
Shall Lead Them

O living truth of God's own Word!
O mystery divine!
A little Child shall lead His own;
A beacon star will shine.

O holy child of Bethlehem,
Thy work will never cease;
Renew our hearts with steadfast faith,
And lead us into peace.

As pilgrims to Thy house of bread,
Our hearts with love aglow;
In humble worship may we kneel
Before Thy manger low.

O angel voices clear and sweet!
O star that shines above!
All praise the child who came to earth
To tell us God is love!

J. HAROLD GWYNNE

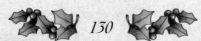

Let Us
Keep Christmas

et us keep Christmas
in the world
And make all
warfare cease
That men may live in brotherhood
And know good will and peace.

Let us keep Christmas in the home
With carol, crèche, and tree,
Reminding us of God's great gift
To all humanity.

Let us keep Christmas in the heart
With faith in God so strong
That we can glimpse the
star of hope
And hear the angels' song.

GAIL BROOK BURKET

Christmas Peace

For unto us a child is born, unto us a son is given: and the government shall be upon his shoulder: and his name shall be called Wonderful, Counsellor, The mighty God, The everlasting Father, The Prince of Peace.

ISAIAH 9:6

Only an Hour

FOR an hour on Christmas Eve
And again on the holy day
Seek the magic of past time,
From this present turn away.
Dark though our day,
Light is the snow on the hawthorn bush,
And the ox knelt down at midnight.

Only an hour, only an hour
From wars and confusions turn away
To the islands of old time
When the world was simple and gay,
Or so we say,
And light lay the snow on the green holly;
The tall oxen knelt at midnight.

Caesar and Herod shared the world,
Sorrow over Bethlehem lay,
Iron the empire, brutal the time,
Dark was the day,
Light lay the snow on the mistletoe berries,
And the oxen knelt down at midnight.

ROBINSON JEFFERS

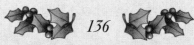

 *137*

Christmas Peace

An Instrument of Thy Peace

Lord, make me an instrument
of Thy peace.
Where there is hatred,
let me sow love;
Where there is injury, pardon;
Where there is doubt, faith;
Where there is despair, hope;
Where there is darkness, light;
When there is sadness, joy.

O divine Master, grant that I
May not so much seek
To be consoled as to console;
Not so much to be understood
As to understand;
Not so much to be loved as to love.
For it is in giving that we receive;
It is in pardoning that we are pardoned;
It is in dying that we awaken to eternal life.

ST. FRANCIS OF ASSISI

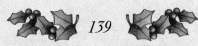

Christmas Peace

Christmas Prayer

O Prince of peace, come now to bless
The whole war-weary earth,
As long ago, when angel choirs
Were heralds of Thy birth.
Forgive us when we place our trust
In armament's mad force
And spurn almighty power which stays
The planets in their course.
Give us the will to use our lives
To serve the common good
That all the peoples of the earth
May know true brotherhood.
Oh, let Thy reign supplant the sword
And turn all hearts to Thee.
Thine is the love which conquers all
And Thine true victory.

GAIL BROOK BURKET

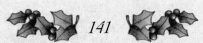

Christmas Peace

O God of Peace

O God of peace,
who hast taught us
that in returning and rest
we shall be saved,
in quietness and in confidence
shall be our strength:
by the might of Thy spirit lift us,
we pray Thee, to Thy presence,
where we may be still and know
that Thou art God;
through Jesus Christ our Lord.
Amen.

BOOK OF COMMON WORSHIP

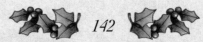

Christmas Peace

A Prayer

Give me, O God,
the understanding heart,
the quick discernment
of the soul to see another's
inner wish, the hidden part of him,
who, wordless,
speaks for sympathy.
I would be kind, but kindness
is not all. In arid places
may I find the wells, the deeps within
my neighbor's soul that call to me
and lead me where his spirit dwells.
When Jesus lifted Mary Magdalene,
and Mary came with alabaster cruse,
a deed was wrought, but more—
there was seen the bond
of holy love of which I muse.
Give me, O God,
the understanding heart
lit with the quickening flame
Thou dost impart.

GEORGIA HARKNESS

Christ Came to Earth

Christ came to earth with a song of peace.
Oh, hear the song, the blessed song.
Christ came to earth
with a song of peace,
Which hearts can hear, if faith be strong.

Christ came to earth with a star of hope.
It brightly gleams, it brightly gleams.
Christ came to earth with a star of hope,
Which lights the world with radiant beams.

Christ came to earth with a gift of love
For all mankind, all mankind.
Christ came to earth with a gift of love
To bless the hearts where love is shrined.

GAIL BROOK BURKET

Christmas Peace

After Bethlehem

After the star and its golden ray,
After the child in the manger bed,
The wise men journeyed a different way,
With new horizons shining ahead.
It is for us as it was for them;
The star is gold, and the child is sweet.
And once we have traveled to Bethlehem,
We lift our eyes and we turn our feet
To roads that we never saw before,
Glory-companioned forevermore!

GRACE V. WATKINS

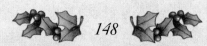

 *149*

Christmas Peace

A Christmas Carol

Before the paling of the stars,
Before the winter morn,
Before the earliest cockcrow,
Jesus Christ was born;
Born in a stable, cradled in a manger,
In the world His hands had made,
Born a stranger.

Priest and king lay fast asleep
In Jerusalem,
Young and old lay fast asleep
In crowded Bethlehem;
Saint and angel, ox and ass,
Kept a watch together,
Before the Christmas daybreak
In the winter weather.

Jesus on His mother's breast,
In the stable cold,
Spotless Lamb of God was He,
Shepherd of the fold:
Let us kneel with Mary maid,
With Joseph, bent and hoary,
With saint and angel, ox and ass,
To hail the King of glory.

CHRISTINA ROSSETTI

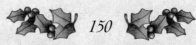

151

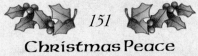

Christmas Peace

Geschenk der

O Strange
Indifference

O strange indifference! Low and high
Drowsed over common joys and cares:
The earth was still—but knew not why;
The world was listening—unawares;
How calm a moment may precede
One that shall thrill the world forever!
To that still moment none would heed,
Man's doom was linked no more to sever,
In the solemn midnight
Centuries ago.

It is the calm and solemn night!
A thousand bells ring out and throw
Their joyous peals abroad, and smile
The darkness, charmed and holy now!
The night that erst no name had worn,
To it a happy name is given;
For in that stable lay newborn
The peaceful Prince of earth and heaven,
In the solemn midnight
Centuries ago.

ALFRED DOMETT

153

Christmas Peace

A Christmas Prayer

Let us pray that strength
and courage abundant be given
to all who work for a world
of reason and understanding;
that the good that lies in each of our hearts
may day by day be magnified;
that we will come to see more clearly
not that which divides us,
but that which unites us;
that each hour may bring us closer
to a final victory, not of nation over nation,
but of ourselves over our own evils
and weaknesses; that the true spirit
of this Christmas season—its joy, its beauty,
its hope, and above all its abiding faith—
may live among us; that the blessing
of peace be ours—the peace to build
and grow, to live in harmony
and sympathy with others,
and to plan for the future
with confidence.

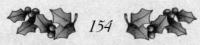

Cadence for Christmas

nce more as chimes break the stillness
In bell-tones melodically clear,
Again we sing carols for Christmas,
Proclaiming His birthday is here.

A tree spills its light through my window
Where frost etchings silver the pane,
As bright as the star that led wise men
To trudge over snow-mounded plain.

They searched for a child in a manger,
In a stable ungraciously bare,
And together with shepherds discovered
New hope for the world shining there.

Once more as chimes break the stillness
And stars wink their crystalline light,
May His love bring the blessings of Christmas
And His presence be with you tonight.

RUBY WATERS ERDELEN

Christmas Wish

May you know the truth of Christmas
That Jesus Christ is King,
Both in a lowly manger
Where heavenly angels sing,
    And on the throne of God
Where hosannas ever ring.

May you know the love of Christmas
Made incarnate on that night
When Jesus came to live on earth
    Bringing hope and light;
Atoning, healing, giving life,
Conquering wrong, enthroning right.

May you know the peace of Christmas
That Christ alone can give,
Not only in your home
And daily as you live,
But hourly, weekly, yearly
And onward to life's eve.

POLLYANNA SEDZIOL

Christmas Blessings

May we not forget the
blessed One
Whose birthday
we rejoice.
May each one have
a quiet time
And place, that we may voice
Our thanks to Him
who sent His Son
Into this world of woe
To teach, to heal,
and at the last
The sacrifice to know.
And, busy as we are with things—
The tinsel, tree, and toys—
May our inmost selves
be gladdened
With much greater
Christmas joys.
For love, transcending
everything,
Keeps homes and hearts as bright
As the star
the wise men followed
That first glorious
Christmas night.

IRENE TAYLOR

INDEX

Ackerlind, Betty Gardner
  "A Season Blest" 49
Adams, Georgia B.
  "At This Time of Year" 89
  "I Must Never Lose the Wonder" 120
Aquinas, Thomas
  "Give Us, O Lord, a Steadfast Heart" 65
Author Unknown
  "A Christmas Prayer" 154
  "Hay, Did You Say?" 46
  "Lord, Increase Our Faith" 56
Bartlett, Robert Merrill
  "Winter" 62
Blake, William
  "A Cradle Song" 12
Book of Common Prayer, The
  "Almighty God, Heavenly Father" 25
  "O Heavenly Father" 28
Book of Common Worship
  "By the Shining of a Star" 101
  "O God of Peace" 142
Buckley, Loretta Bauer
  "May You Know Joy" 8
  "On This Hallowed Eve
    of Christmas" 122
Buckwalter, Esther S.
  "One Small Child" 39
Burgess, Joy Belle
  "Christmas Prayer" 35
Burket, Gail Brook
  "Christ Came to Earth" 146
  "Christmas Prayer" 141
  "Let Us Keep Christmas" 132
Carmichael, Amy
  "For Our Children" 22
  "Winter" 68
Clark, Thomas Curtis
  "The Christmas Hope" 85
Crowell, Grace Noll
  "A Christmas Prayer" 82
  "Joseph" 15
  "The Road to Christmas" 78
Dauber, Esther L.
  "There Will Be Christmas" 21

Day, Myrtle Beeler
  "Lord, Bless the Cards We've Written" ... 104
Domett, Alfred
  "O Strange Indifference" 153
Doncaster, Jr., William Trall
  "Not What I Hold" 29
Erdelen, Ruby Waters
  "Cadence for Christmas" 156
Field, Ruth B.
  "Gift of Gifts" 114
Freeman, James Dillet
  "Make Me a Blessing" 36
Goodman, Chleo Deshler
  "The Shepherd" 58-59
Guest, Edgar A.
  "A Christmas Carol" 51
  "A Christmas Wish" 45
  "I Do Not Ask of Thee" 16
Gwynne, J. Harold
  "Christmas: Another Way" 93
  "A Little Child Shall Lead Them" 130
Harkness, Georgia
  "A Prayer" 144
Haynes, Laura Baker
  "A Christmas Tree Prayer" 27
Herrick, Robert
  "To His Saviour, A Child:
    A Present by a Child" 111
Hopkins, Gerard Manley
  "Moonless Darkness" 90
Jeffers, Robinson
  "Only an Hour" 136
Kratowicz, Nancy L.
  "The Gift" 102
L'Engle, Madeleine
  "O Simplicitas" 11
Love, Adelaide
  "Later Christmas Eves" 60
  "Lord Jesus, You Who Bade
    the Children Come" 18
Lutz, Anna D.
  "Christmas Praise" 127
Marshall, Peter
  "The Day after Christmas" 30-31

"For Christmas the Year Round" 53
"For a Renaissance of Faith" 74
"On a Winter's Day" 115
"The Wondrous Spell of Christmas" 7
Matthews, Kathy
  "Guide Our Steps" 97
Merchant, Jane
  "A Prayer" 71
  "We Thank Thee, Heavenly Father" 109
Morgan, Lola S.
  "The Wise Men's Story" 81
Newman, John Henry
  "Lead, Kindly Light" 72
Roddy, Florence Howery
  "A Christmas Dream" 86
Rorke, Margaret
  "Ponderings" 41
Rossetti, Christina
  "A Christmas Carol" 150
Sedziol, Pollyanna
  "A Christmas Wish" 157
Silesius, Angelus
  "Paradox" 124
Smith, Anna B.
  "Gifts of Love" 113
St. Francis of Assisi
  "An Instrument of Thy Peace" 139
Stevenson, Robert Louis
  "A Christmas Prayer" 42
Stoffel, Betty W.
  "The Returning Christ" 94
Sutton, Louise Weibert
  "A Christmas Blessing" 116
Taylor, Irene
  "Christmas Blessings" 159
Tennyson, Alfred, Lord
  "Ring Out, Wild Bells" 128-129
Turner, Nancy Byrd
  "Let This Be Borne in Every Heart" 107
Watkins, Grace V.
  "After Bethlehem" 148
Wells, Amos Russell
  "The Inn: The Landlord
    Speaks A.D. 28" 66-67

PHOTOGRAPHY CREDITS

Page 4: *The Annunciation* by Leonardo Da Vinci; Superstock. **6:** Ohio River, Fredonia, Indiana; Adam Jones. **9:** Crested Butte, Colorado; Steve Terrill. **10:** Lake Gerold, West Germany; M. Thonig/H. Armstrong Roberts. **13:** St. Joseph's, Hammond, Indiana; Gene Plaisted, OSC/The Crosiers. **14:** B. Taylor/H. Armstrong Roberts. **17:** Winema National Forest, Oregon; Steve Terrill. **19:** Deschutes National Forest, Oregon; Jon Gnass. **20:** D. Petku/H. Armstrong Roberts. **23:** *The Annunciation* by Guilio Cesare Procaccini; Superstock. **24:** Shelby County, Kentucky; Adam Jones. **26:** Mt. Hood National Forest, Oregon; H. Richard Johnston/FPG. **32:** *The New Born Child* by Georges De La Tour; Superstock. **34:** Silver Falls State Park, Oregon; Steve Terrill. **37:** Saint John's Lutheran, Wilimette, Illinois; P. Pearson/H. Armstrong Roberts. **38:** Mt. Hood National Forest, Oregon; Steve Terrill. **40:** Sacred Heart Church, Eau Claire, Wisconsin; Gene Plaisted, OSC/The Crosiers. **43:** Daniel Boone National Forest, Kentucky; Adam Jones. **44:** Maroon Creek, Aspen, Colorado; Ron Thomas/FPG. **47:** *Adoration of the Shepherds* by Jacob Jordaens; Superstock. **48:** Salmon-Huckleberry Wilderness, Oregon; Steve Terrill. **50:** Mt. Hood National Forest, Oregon; Steve Terrill. **52:** New Hampshire; W. Pote/H. Armstrong Roberts. **54:** *Adoration of the Shepherds* by Robert Leinweber; Superstock. **56:** Stark, New Hampshire; G. Ahrens/H. Armstrong Roberts. **61:** Mt. Hood National Forest, Oregon; Steve Terrill. **63:** Ohio River, Fredonia, Indiana; Adam Jones. **64:** *The Birth of Christ* by Domenico Ghirlandaio; Superstock. **69:** Sangre de Cristo mountains, San Isabel National Forest, Colorado; Jeff Gnass. **70:** H. Armstrong Roberts. **73:** Bavaria; E. Nagele/FPG. **75:** Lincoln Cathedral, Lincoln, England; Gene Plaisted, OSC/The Crosiers. **76:** *Adoration of the Magi* by Fra Angelico; Superstock. **78:** Cotswolds, Gloucestershire, England; FPG. **80:** St. Peter's Church, North St. Paul, Minnesota; Gene Plaisted, OSC/The Crosiers. **83:** H. Lefebvre/H. Armstrong Roberts. **84:** Oregon; M. Thonig/H. Armstrong Roberts. **86:** Mendenhall Glacier and Towers on Auke Lake, Mendenhall Valley, Alaska; Jeff Gnass. **88:** *The Nativity* by Benvenuto Di Giovanni Guasta; Superstock. **90:** Deschutes National Forest, Oregon; Steve Terrill. **92:** B. Taylor/H. Armstrong Roberts. **94:** Superstock. **96:** Mt. Hood National Forest, Oregon; Steve Terrill. **98:** *Adoration of the Kings* by Peter Paul Rubens; Superstock. **100:** Missouri; Gay Bumgarner. **103:** *Nativity* by L. Vernansal; Superstock. **105:** American Cranberry Bush, Missouri; Gay Bumgarner. **106:** Whitetail Deer; Neal and Mary Jane Mishler/FPG. **108:** El Capitan Reflects in Merced River, Yosemite National Park, California; Jeff Gnass. **110:** Sacred Heart Seminary, Detroit, Michigan; Gene Plaisted, OSC/The Crosiers. **112:** Crater Lake National Park, Oregon; Jeff Gnass. **117:** New Hampshire; A. Griffin/H. Armstrong Roberts. **118:** *The Adoration of the Shepherds* by Bartolome Esteban Murillo; Superstock. **121:** Louisville, Kentucky; Adam Jones. **123:** Kootznoowoo Wilderness, Tongass National Forest, Alaska; Jeff Gnass. **125:** Carlisle Cathedral, Carlisle, England; Gene Plaisted, OSC/The Crosiers. **126:** Mt. Hood National Forest, Oregon; Steve Terrill. **131:** *Adoration of the Magi* by Bernardino Luini; Superstock. **132:** Clackamas County, Oregon; Steve Terrill. **134:** *The Nativity* by Gerrit van Honthorst; Superstock. **137:** Chamonix, France; Telegraph Colour Library/FPG. **138:** H. Armstrong Roberts. **140:** Male Cardinal; Gay Bumgarner. **143:** Sawtooth National Forest, Idaho; Jon Gnass. **145:** Grand Canyon from Hopi Point, Arizona; Josiah Davidson. **146:** Zefa-U.K./H. Armstrong Roberts. **149:** Mountain Ash Berries, Mt. Rainier National Park, Washington; Adam Jones. **150:** Mt. Ashland in Rogue River National Forest, Oregon; Steve Terrill. **152:** Immaculate Conception Church, New Munich, Minnesota; Gene Plaisted, OSC/The Crosiers. **155:** Oak Creek Canyon Near Sedona, Arizona; Josiah Davidson. **158:** *Adoration of the Shepherds* by Guido Reni; Superstock.